BECOME YOUR TRUE SELF

5 Proven Techniques to Overcome Your Fear and Shyness

Wright Chase
Award-Winning Author

10-10-10 Publishing

Publisher
10-10-10 Publishing
Markham, ON
Canada

Contents

I dedicate this book to every person who is fearful and shy,
to overcome it, and gain control of your awesome life!

Foreword

Become Your True Self by Wright Chase is a guide to the struggles of fear and shyness that you may be facing today, including five proven techniques the author has found that will help you to overcome it. Wright reminds you that if you challenge yourself to be the best, change is inevitable.

Wright takes you on his journey with detail and color that makes *Become Your True Self* both informative and fun. His transparency is honest and painful, yet giving. He touches on points that will make you look deeply at yourself.

Wright does not just talk about his successes; he pulls you into his life of hardship and doubt, shows you how he transformed himself and how you can too. It is rare to find an author who is so blunt and honest about his techniques, but Wright is just that. His willingness to share such private struggles in his own life is a testament to his desire for you to win.

This book is a powerful life-changer, so I strongly encourage you read it from cover to cover. No matter where you are in life today, this book can make you better. I got great pleasure from this book, and I believe you will too.

Raymond Aaron
New York Times Bestselling Author

Acknowledgements

I would first like to thank my mom, **Elenore Chase**, for raising me to be the person that I am today. I always would look up to her, and still do, because she is always able to talk to anyone, know exactly what to say, how to say it, and make everyone feel happy and comfortable. I would not have been able to achieve all my successes if not for the endless love, admiration, guidance, and patience that she has given me.

I would like to thank my dad, **Roscoe Jack Chase**, for his patience, respect, and wisdom, and for his support of me. We had many great conversations about current events, school, and church happenings, while I was growing up; and, of course, we also had the laughs. I wish he was still around so that I could show him this book in person, but I postulate he is looking down on me with a smile on his face.

To my sons, **Andrew Chase** and **Matthew Chase**, who both are Eagle Scouts and have shown the same patience, respect, wisdom, and support as their grandfather had. It is the love of a parent for their children that motivates them to take on challenges, to be their best *true self,* and to put them on a better path. You both have inspired me to manifest my own *true self,* and to strive for perfection.

I am extremely grateful to one of the most amazing people in the whole world, **Daphne Dickens-King**, for her leadership and unparalleled ability to help others. Her insights have helped me to view situations more clearly and find opportunities to create WOW experiences. I am so honored to be able to call her my friend.

I am also so grateful for all my clients that I have met through speaking and workshops. A teacher cannot teach without students. For most of my adult life, I am constantly thankful that so many eager people want to learn from me. WOW!

Last but not least, I deeply acknowledge the wisdom and friendship of **Martin Sussman**, and his leadership and insight for decades of creating and running his own businesses. He is always overly eager to help, help, help—no matter what. I am deeply moved by his dedication to make the world a better place.

Chapter 1

The End of Your Old Life

"Shyness makes up almost half of the population, and about 95% of us know first-hand what it means to be shy in some situations."
— Dr. Bernardo Carducci

Have you ever had the experience where you knew the answer to a question asked in a class—OR—you had a great idea in a meeting at work, but no matter how much you wanted to raise your hand and speak out, there was just something holding you back?

Or maybe you are minding your own business, walking down the hallway or down a busy street, and you see, from afar, someone you know. You see them, but they have not seen you yet, and suddenly you activate your disappearing act, as you strategically reroute your path to avoid an awkward conversation.

What about when you are introduced to a friend of a friend, and you have absolutely no idea what you're going to say, after "Hi, nice to meet you?" So you look back at your friend, with a desperate expression that screams, "Help Me!"

You definitely are not alone, my friend. Those experiences were not just occasional things for me while growing up; they were a part of my daily routine during my childhood and young adult life. But here is the thing: those awkward social scenarios that I referred to were not just uncomfortable—they were extremely painful.

My stomach would tighten up, and I would literally exhaust myself by overanalyzing and critiquing everything that I did or said. Since those feelings and thoughts were a daily occurrence, I rationalized in my head that this was just who I was and how it was going to be.

But you and I both know this book is not about me; it is about you and your future. When fearful and shy people hear that statistic by Dr. Bernardo Carducci, at the beginning of this chapter, I hear the same response: "I thought it was just me!" I responded the same way too, the first time I saw it.

Many other people, as diverse and successful as Robert Frost, Eleanor Roosevelt, Bob Dole, Al Gore, Carol Burnett, Barbara Walters, Johnny Carson, David Letterman, Barbara Hershey, Jennifer Jason Leigh, Sting, Prince Albert of Monaco, and the late Princess Diana—the smart, the bold, the beautiful, the rich, the royal, and the famous—have all identified themselves as shy and fearful.

So, I want to share with you the exact steps I have taken throughout my journey, to help you overcome your fear and shyness, improve your social skills, and most importantly, express more of *your true self*. And this is why I named this chapter, *The End of Your Old Life.*

Whether you are an introvert or extrovert, loud or quiet, reserved or open, it does not matter. The principles and path I am going to lay out in this book, which I have taught through my workshops, will help you stand apart from the crowd, make more friends, and feel more comfortable in your own skin!

So, what are we waiting for? Let's get started! But first, you need to know...

What to Expect

The first half of this book will be your chance to go within and begin to strengthen your mindset by understanding what has been holding you back, how to create lasting change, and how to start focusing on your exciting new future.

During this section, I will be opening up and sharing with you my own journey; and then explaining each principle and how it can be applied to your life. I do this to demonstrate that these are not simply theories that I have read about or researched. I have lived them, and I know they have the power to provide the same benefits for you.

The second half of the book is when it starts to get really exciting. I will be sharing with you the best techniques and practices that you can use out in the real world to build your confidence and start applying these practical social skills.

I will refer to these as *Your True Self Tips,* because you can pull them out anytime, anywhere. You can use them to spark up and enjoy a friendly conversation and, potentially, make a new friend.

When you use one of these techniques, you may notice a little confidence boost and pep in your step afterwards. Embrace it. Other times, it may feel awkward and uncomfortable—especially at first— and that is completely normal. Embrace it.

True Self vs. False Self

There is one more thing you should know before we dive in with both feet into this journey together. Throughout this book, I will often refer to you and *your true self.*

The opposite, of course, is your *false self.* I believe that you and I are behaving as our *false self* whenever we believe in the thoughts that make us feel anxious, fearful, judgmental, lonely, stressed, worried, or in constant need of validation.

Our *true self* is when we are aligned with the thoughts that make us feel worthy, loved, accepted, thankful, relaxed, connected, honest, forgiving, trusting, or at peace.

Your true self is not a reference to any religious practice but rather a state of mind in which you feel good and connected with the core of what makes you human.

So, now that you are warmed up and stretched out, let's move on to...

The Four-Letter Word

Fear.

David Icke, author and renowned public speaker, has quoted, *"The greatest prison people live in is the fear of what other people think."*

Many people form opinions about what they know nothing about— including you and me—and act like they are authorities on the subject. So, why should we fear other people's opinions and comments? I spent years being afraid of talking to other people out of fear of their disapproval.

But I eventually discovered that most people were not judging and critiquing me at all as I thought they were; those few who did, really are losers who will think and talk negative about anyone and anything. I was trapped in my own mind because of fear.

This is why the quote by David Ives, at the beginning of this sub-section, is so powerful and true. Go back and reread it!

Why Fear and Shyness Go Hand in Hand

Fear has become so embedded in our nervous systems because, thousands of years ago—I am talking caveman days—it was an extremely important and useful emotional response. It was an internal warning sign, which would protect our ancestors from the saber-toothed tigers that were trying to make them their dinner.

In the modern world, we still have the same emotional trigger in our bodies; it is just that a hungry beast is not hunting us. Most of our social fears stem from the caveman days.

Back then, if you were rejected and shunned by the tribe, it was a death sentence. You either died of starvation or from the elements, or you became some predator's meal.

We no longer live in tribes or depend on them for physical survival. Unfortunately, we are still hardwired to belong to a group and fear rejection. These fears are totally irrational. Today, if someone rejects us, nothing happens. We are totally safe. We know this logically, but our brains are still hardwired to equate rejection with death.

Rejection does not feel nice, but that is not enough to cause paralyzing fear. This is our brain's way of keeping us safe from something it perceives to be a real threat to our survival, because it is still operating in *caveman mode*.

In most scenarios—for quiet people like you and me—fear of rejection comes up when we are meeting someone new, giving a speech in public, being interviewed for a job, or maybe even simply answering a phone call.

It is important to understand that fear is not something external. We cannot pick it up, pack it tight, lock it up in a box, and throw away the key, in efforts to get rid of it. It comes from within. It is even more important to realize, because you are a quiet or shy person, you probably have a very powerful imagination.

Our active imagination can either serve as our best friend or our worst enemy. We can use it to create a highlight reel of all the times we felt awkward and uncomfortable around other people, or we can envision ourselves meeting someone new, boldly shaking their hand, looking them in the eye, and making an amazing first impression.

So, how do we effectively channel that adrenaline and racing heartbeat when fear is triggered in our minds? We have to make an internal shift ...

Stop Looking in Your Mirror

One of my favorite classes in college was—go figure—a public speaking course. It was way outside of my comfort zone. The professor was an exuberant man, and he taught us with immersion, not just boring lectures talking about theories and history.

Within the first week of the class, he had us do an exercise that I will never forget. One by one, he challenged each of us to stand up in front of the class and give two, one-minute, *me* presentations, sharing who we are and our backgrounds.

The first time each person got up, he gave him or her a giant mirror that reflected the person's face for the full minute. I am not sure who felt more uncomfortable each time someone did this—the presenter or the audience.

When it was my turn, and I started talking with the giant mirror reflecting back to me, I could only notice how my hair was a mess, and the faces I was making. Of course, I bombed it big time, just like everyone else. Yikes!

The second time around, the mirror was turned around the other way, so we could not see ourselves. As you can imagine, the energy in the room was completely different this time. Each presentation was much smoother, and everyone was way more comfortable.

After everyone had presented twice, he went on to explain that when the mirror was in front of us—either real or imaginary—we only focused on ourselves. We predominately think about how we look and how others perceive us. We are critical and judgmental. As a result, when our mirror is in, we are much less effective as communicators.

When we flip the mirror around, however, we have the ability to focus all of our attention and energy on other people and our environment. Once our mirror is out, we are free to connect with the world around us.

Do you go throughout your daily routine with your mirror in, or out? Are you trapped in your head, or are you living in the present moment? While someone else is talking, are you thinking about what you are going to say next? It is okay if you do this. It does not make you crazy; it means you are human, and you have room to grow.

The very first step is to start becoming aware of where you decide to focus. Remember, when our mirror is in, we are consumed with fear. When our mirror is out, we are then able to tap into our potential. In the next chapter, I will be explaining to you the real secrets of mindset. When you see the answers, you will be blown away.

Be sure to visit YourTrueSelfBook.com, and click on FREE BOOK
BONUSES to receive several valuable gifts, which include:

A full page, full color, print-ready copy of all *Your True Self Tips*.
A full page, full color, print-ready action plan!
The book, *Become Your True Self*, on audio, read by the author!

* Please note that the bonus offerings may change.

Notes

Notes

Notes

Chapter 2

The Mindset

"If you want to do something big in your life, you must remember that shyness is only the mind. If you think shy, you act shy. If you think confident, you act confident. Therefore, never let shyness conquer your mind."
– Arfa Karim

Another interesting statistic, as Dr. Bernardo Carducci states, is that upwards of 15% of the population are born shy. And I will be the first one to admit that I am one of them. Born in 1960, and raised in the western suburbs of Chicago, I would not say *boo* to anyone. You could tell from all the pictures taken when I was growing up: I was always looking down.

It did not help back then that all the children had common names (e.g., Brian, Matthew, Steven, Bruce, Charles, Michael, Robert, etc.), except for me. Nowadays, names are unique; but back then, the unique name, Wright, brought with it—left and right—jokes.

I do get asked many times today how I got the name, *Wright.* I was named after my great-grandfather, which I have well documented: framed on my desk, in my office, is his official discharge paper from the Civil War. And it is officially signed by the President of the United States at that time: Andrew Johnson. Everyone has a big- time WOW about it, including me.

Lastly, I still remember when I was in 4th grade, and my eyesight went south very quickly. I still recall the day when my mother asked me why I was squinting at the TV. Back then, they did not have the cool frames and featherweight lenses like they have today—they were all ugly, black frames, with huge, ungodly lenses.

They looked terrible. And, of course, the jokes from the kids were flying left and right, which made me crawl into my shell even more.

Well, all these jokes and bullying kept on throughout my public school years, adding to my fear and shyness. Life started to turn for me after I started college. New surroundings, new people—and since students were there for a purpose of making or bettering a life for themselves, they were not there to pick on a student like me.

I had a professor during my first semester, who sensed, of course, that I was fearful and shy; so, he told me about a book that I should read, which was in the school library. I did not know it was one of those (self-help) books, and if I did, I probably would not have read it.

The weird thing was, up to this time in my life, I hated to read any book, but this one was different, and I could not put it down. I do not think my head stopped nodding up and down, like a bobble head, as a scrolled through each page. As I learned about this gentleman's story and internal battles, it occurred to me that, maybe, I was not the only one feeling isolated and disconnected from the world.

If this guy, who was a TV celebrity and best-selling author, experienced the same negative thoughts, self-doubt, and insecurities that I was feeling, then there had to be others like me as well.

A Shift in Perspective

In the book, this gentleman talked about how each person has around 60,000 thoughts per day. Sixty thousand! WOW, that blew me away! And then it scared me. I estimated that at least 75% of my thoughts consisted of...

- Why am I so shy?
- There is something wrong with me.
- I should not have said that.
- Someday, I will...
- Why am I so awkward?
- I should have said something.
- I wish I were more confident.
- If only I were like...

Then something clicked. If this celebrity had those same negative thoughts about his anxiety, and he changed, why couldn't I change? I just had to do what he did. This began to strengthen a belief in me: what is possible for one is possible for all.

During this process, there would be times when I would envision what my life would be like once my shyness was no longer in the driver's seat. I would see myself being social, and it felt incredible to imagine that freedom.

I was also slowly becoming obsessed with this idea of personal development. Reading a book for class, about biology or chemistry, bored me to tears. But if I picked up a book that taught me how to control my emotions and strengthen my mindset, I could not put it down.

I began to believe—for the first time—that I really could reprogram my mind. I started to think of my brain as a computer. There were inputs and outputs that just needed to be adjusted.

Although I was starting to feel better on the inside, my life did not look much different from the outside. I did not feel comfortable telling many people about these new little tricks I had been picking up, but I could feel a shift starting to build up. I had no idea that the biggest turning of point my life was just around the corner.

Why Am I Not Living to My Fullest Potential?

I think we both can agree that every human has the same amount of potential. We all may have grown up in different parts of the world, with different families that raised us; and we may have received different educations, but with a functioning brain and a heart that still beats, we all have the ability to become whatever we put our minds to.

So, why do people continue to have more, give more, and become more, while others have a tough time keeping their heads above water and constantly struggle? Why do some people exude confidence while others feel more and more awkward as the days go by?

The answer became clear when I first saw Tony Robbins' flow chart about what he calls his *success cycle,* which states that *Potential* leads to *Action,* which produces *Results,* which reinforces *Beliefs.* This cycle can be used in any area of our lives to either build us up or tear us down.

Before I had my breakthrough, which I will talk about in the next chapter, I was using the cycle in a very unsuccessful way with my fear and shyness. Here is what it looked like for me...

Potential – I would remind myself daily that since I had always been a shy and reserved person, I would always be like that. I was born that way; it is genetic, and there is nothing I could do. That is just the way it is.

Action – I rarely introduced myself or tried to make new friends. I would sit near the back of the class and pray that I would not be noticed, and I chose the shifts at work where I would be isolated, with the least amount of interaction as possible.

Result – I would get extremely uncomfortable and would not know what to say in daily conversations.

Belief – My brain would say, "See, I told you that you are awkward and shy."

Wash, rinse, and repeat. That would strengthen my belief in fear, so I would live out my own self-fulfilling prophecy. Having this belief was detrimental to my growth.

Because I believed I was inherently fearful and shy, I rarely bothered trying to change it. And when I did try to overcome my shyness, and it did not work, that just confirmed my belief that something was inherently wrong with me or it was a genetic fault in my brain.

What is the Solution?

As much as I wish I could, it is simply not possible for me to give you more potential, make you take more action, give you better results, or strengthen your belief in yourself. Luckily, the obstacle that has been holding you back from expressing *your true self,* is also your opportunity.

I share with you my story of hitting rock bottom, at the beginning of this chapter, because it is in moments like that, when we decide enough is enough, that we actually start to make change.

It would be great if we could sit around and wait until the day came that suddenly we magically developed a confidence muscle and were instantly more comfortable around people. But you and I both know that life is not like that. The answers to all of your problems already live within you—you just need to bring them to the surface.

Using Your Imagination

Whether you realize it or not, your mind is constantly envisioning—and creating— what your future is going to be. What you and I are going to do together is to start replacing more positive images than negative ones in your mind's highlight reel. We must become certain in our mind about who we are becoming, long before it actually happens.

Have you heard the story of Roger Bannister? Before 1954, no one had ever run a mile in less than four minutes. It was believed by most that the task was simply impossible. Up until that year, the fastest time recorded was 4:01, and the general consensus was that the human body wasn't designed to run any faster than that.

The difference between Roger and the rest of the world was that he was certain that he could do it, and he would imagine himself crossing the finish line in less than four minutes. His opportunity came on May 6, 1954, when he finished with a time of 3:59:4, and he became the first man to ever break the four-minute barrier.

The amazing part of this story is that 46 days later, another man broke the four-minute mark, and since that day, thousands of people have run a four-minute mile, including many high school athletes.

I am not asking you to run a mile in less than four minutes. Nor am I suggesting you become a TV celebrity or professional public speaker. What I am asking and challenging you to do is to be open to the idea of believing in your potential of what is possible, by visualizing yourself as the person you want to become.

Several scientific studies have proven the positive benefits of visualization. The late Dr. Maxwell Maltz, author of the book, *Psycho-Cybernetics*, stated that if a person's imagination is vivid and detailed enough, it tricks their nervous system into thinking that what they visualize is actually real.

If, every day, you give yourself at least 5–10 minutes to visualize yourself being the confident person you want to become, it will become easier for you to act that way in public.

When you visualize, you are drafting a blueprint of the person you want to become. You are experiencing what it feels like to act confidently in a social situation. Then, when it actually happens, it is easier because you have already rehearsed the scenario in your mind and know what it feels like.

This is how you can prepare for a social event, because you have already done it in your mind and visualized it going well.

Many other people believed in me before I believed in myself, and now I am asking you to make room for the person you want to become; and you will have your own breakthrough. In the next chapter, we will be explaining this breakthrough even further. Keep reading to find out how.

Be sure to visit YourTrueSelfBook.com, and click on FREE BOOK BONUSES to receive several valuable gifts, which include:

A full page, full color, print-ready copy of all *Your True Self Tips.*
A full page, full color, print-ready action plan!
The book, *Become Your True Self,* on audio, read by the author!

* Please note that the bonus offerings may change.

Notes

Notes

Chapter 3

Ready, Set, GO

"You have two choices: to control your mind
or to let your mind control you."
– Paulo Coelho

Six months had gone by after reading that book, recommended by my professor, and my life looked... pretty much the same. I was feeling a little bit better from the new healthy habits I was developing. Yet, despite these subtle changes, I was still scared to talk to people.

I had no idea I was about to experience my first major breakthrough in life. Then it happened.

It was a day just like any other. I was working, and then, for some strange reason and in an instant, I experienced a jolt of energy that rushed through my body. I started initiating conversations with my co-workers and the customers. I was smiling, laughing, asking questions, giving compliments, and making new friends. It was exhilarating!

But where was this coming from? I did not give myself enough time to ponder that question—like I usually would have done—and went with the flow. The next four hours flew by, and my shift was coming to an end, but I did not want this to stop. I was having more fun than I had in a long time.

By the time I got home and had a chance to reflect, it was awesome. I experienced a natural high from in-depth conversations, and I knew my life would never be the same. I was hooked.

The rest of that year was truly transformative. Each new day, new person, and new conversation was an opportunity to learn and challenge my fear. I began making new friends at work and in my classes. These were people who I saw almost every day but was always too afraid to go beyond small talk with.

I started going to parties and having fun, and went on adventures around the city. I was open to anything and everything, but I felt most alive from simply enjoying long, honest conversations with new friends.

For the first time, I was excited about going to work and class. The story in my mind was slowly shifting from, "I am so awkward and weird, and will always be shy," to, "I have nothing to lose! Life is too short to hide in my little shell, and I actually really enjoy talking to people!"

I started to believe that maybe—just maybe—I could overcome this fear and shyness that has held me back for so long. My mother was a people-person, and I always wanted to be more like her in that way, and this was the first time that I started to think that it was possible.

A new question started entering my mind each day, which I had never thought of before: "What else am I afraid of?" I rationalized that if I could conquer this fear of opening up and talking, I could do anything. I started to bring those fears to the surface and went after them one by one. All of my self-constructed obstacles started to become opportunities.

You and Your Breakthrough

By now, I hope you are thinking, "Okay, this is all great, but how am I going to overcome my fear and shyness?" Whether it is overcoming shyness, expressing more of *your true self,* improving your social skills, or literally any other area of your life, a breakthrough is what will take your life to the next level.

One more thing before we dissect how to create your breakthrough—I said it before, and I will say it again—this book is about taking action! Otherwise, you will continue to bounce around from book to book, seminar to seminar, opportunity to opportunity, always looking for an answer, when the answer is already inside of you. So let us bring it to life.

What exactly is a breakthrough? A breakthrough is the moment you declare, "I can never go back to who I was," and you begin to embrace your new path.

Chances are good that you have already experienced at least one major breakthrough in your life. Maybe it was when you decided you would never smoke another cigarette or eat fast food. Maybe it was when you forgave someone you had been holding a grudge against for years. Whatever it was, something shifted in you, and your life will never be the same.

Understanding the Power of Your Story

We all have a story circulating in our minds about who we are and what we are capable of. To have a voice in your mind does not make you crazy; it makes you human. That story that you carry with yourself each day is shaping your perception of the world.

I can, and will, give you strategies and techniques to come out of your shell and become a confident communicator; but if the story in the back of your mind keeps repeating, "Yeah, but this is just not for me; it may work for others but not for me," then you will remain stuck until you change your story.

The difference between those who are social, outgoing, and confident in everyday conversations, compared to those who feel timid, insecure, and reserved, simply comes down to the thoughts that each person believes in with absolute certainty.

What is the story that is penetrating in your mind? Is it empowering you, or does it bring you down? Does it give you energy, or make you want to hide? If your best friend talked to you the way you talk to yourself, would you still want to be their friend?

As I shared earlier, the never-ending thoughts in my mind at that time were, "I am shy and awkward; people think I am weird; and I had better not speak up and make a fool of myself!" Whether these thoughts were true or not was completely up to me, so I was living my self-fulfilling prophecy.

To change the story in my mind, I started practicing a technique through thinking. I would observe my thoughts as though they were clouds passing through my head. If the clouds made me feel good, I would let them stick around. If they did not feel good, I would let them float on by and out my ear. We become the thoughts that we consistently focus on and attach our emotions to.

Instead of repeating in your mind, "I just do not want to be fearful and shy anymore," I am challenging you to focus on what you want, not what you do not want. When that thought-cloud that says, "I am a social person, and it is easy for me to make friends," sneaks into your mind, make space for it, and let it hang out for a while.

Energize Your Thoughts

Just like the stories that shape our perception, our daily energy level, or state of mind, creates how we interpret the world around us. It is difficult to act confident and strike up a conversation if you are feeling timid and afraid. You will psyche yourself out before you even have a chance.

Think about your mind as if it were a thermostat. Let us say that over the years, you have found that you feel comfortable setting your thermostat at 72°F (22°C). Now, every day, good things happen, which makes your internal temperature rise up, and bad things will happen, which causes a drop in temperature. But you always find a way back to your comfortable, laid-back 72°F (22°C).

To overcome your fear and shyness with higher energy when talking to people, you are going to need to manually reset your thermostat to 75°F (24°C). That will take effort. Your mind is not going to like this because that is not what it is habitually used to, and it will feel uncomfortable at first.

Guess what? You control your thermostat. It does not control you.

How do we control our energy level? With our bodies. Positive emotion is created by motion. All of the latest research will agree that we can change our biochemistry and philosophy by movement.

Do not get me wrong; I am not suggesting that you should start doing jumping jacks before you shake someone's hand and start a conversation—unless that is your thing. I am suggesting that you start creating daily habits that get your body moving and put you in a heightened state of mind each day.

You and I both know that trying to talk ourselves into doing something just does not work. We have got to move the body and energize our thoughts. The goal is to become aware of when your energy level starts to drop, and to find your strategy to bring it back up on a daily, moment-to-moment basis.

Putting It All Together

Your breakthrough will come when you have a heightened state of mind, with a new, exciting story that you believe in.

Remember what we talked about at the beginning of this chapter: it happens in a moment. The cool part is that you get to decide when that moment happens. It can literally occur as soon as you put this book down, or it can happen a year from now, when you finally give yourself permission to change. The decision is up to you, and as you do, you will start expanding your identity.

Start reading the next chapter now to discover the secret advantage.

Be sure to visit YourTrueSelfBook.com, and click on FREE BOOK BONUSES to receive several valuable gifts, which include:

A full page, full color, print-ready copy of all *Your True Self Tips*.
A full page, full color, print-ready action plan!
The book, *Become Your True Self,* on audio, read by the author!

* Please note that the bonus offerings may change.

Notes

Notes

Notes

Chapter 4

Get Out of Your Comfort Zone

*"The sooner you step away from your comfort zone, the sooner
you'll realize that it really wasn't all that comfortable."*
– Eddie Harris Jr.

We talked a lot so far about all these changes that you are seeking, experimenting with, or will be experimenting with soon, in the pursuit of overcoming your fear and shyness. Let us not forget that change is inevitable no matter what. What we are really after is growth and expansion to become more of *your true self.*

I do not think there is anything wrong with you in the first place, and I do not want you to trick yourself into believing that there is. This journey is not about you changing your identity; it is about expanding your identity.

This is about bringing out the social, playful, passionate person that you are, and that requires digging past the fears, discovering your potential, and experiencing your breakthrough to get there.

The Freedom to Be Yourself

I remember thinking after my breakthrough that I can be whoever I want to be. No one there knows who I have been. This is incredible!

Have you ever had that feeling? It is empowering and exciting to know that you can create a new life for yourself at any time. It does not require transferring schools or moving to somewhere new—all we need to do is make the decision and commit.

The biggest surprise from that experience was a passion that I never knew I had, and I doubt I ever would have realized it if I had not tried new things and expanded outside of my comfort zone.

If you want to become more confident and achieve your goals in life, sooner or later, you are going to have to get out of your comfort zone and put yourself in situations where you can potentially be rejected, but from which you will always grow and learn.

Robert Allen, author of the *One Minute Millionaire,* wrote, *"Everything you want in your life is just outside your comfort zone."*

Getting out of your comfort zone is when the real magic happens in your life. Yes, it can be painful and uncomfortable at times, but it is like getting into a cold shower. When you finally take the plunge, the water stings for a few seconds, but then you get used to it and actually start to like it. Then, afterwards, you feel awake and refreshed.

It is exactly the same with trying new things, getting out of your comfort zone, and expanding your identity. During my public speaking class in college, the professor asked each student to give a little pep talk to the rest of the class each week. To be honest, it scared the living daylights out of me. So, of course, since it scared me and was way outside my comfort zone, I decided to give it a go.

During that first pep talk, as I opened up and shared what had led me to take the class, I felt my spirit come to life, and I was absolutely energized by the challenge. That morning, I discovered my passion for inspiring others through stories.

Before that day, if you would have told me that I was going to become a public speaker, I would have called you crazy and checked you into a mental hospital for treatment. Maybe you already know what you are most passionate about or what your life's calling is. Or maybe you feel like you are running around in circles with no direction or purpose.

If you believe your fear and shyness has been holding you back, then it is time for us to get to work. Let us dig deeper to bring out more of *your true self.*

Bringing Out the Best of You

Since your goal here is to no longer be fearful and/or shy, then we need to start thinking about what your life will be like when you are confident. I believe that you have talents, insight, and skills within you that you are not even aware of yet.

The main way that you are going to bring your uniqueness to life is by setting exciting goals and heading in a new direction. If all we can think about is overcoming fear and shyness, we will stay trapped in that lower level of energy and fail to rise up to the next level. Once we start to focus on more of what we want, our brain begins to find the answers for us.

My whole life started to change, and I discovered confidence in my social skills once I began to follow and trust my heart, and I am absolutely certain that the same can happen for you once you decide to follow yours.

Goal Setting That Makes Sense

You are going to enjoy this section because I am giving you permission to dream like you used to dream when you were a kid. It is very important to go through this exercise with a no-limits attitude. Think in terms of what you really want, not merely what you believe is possible. Inspired ideas and actions come from inspiring dreams; so dream big, and do not hold back.

You are going to have a lot of fun with this, but before you start, make sure you are in a *great* state of mind—not a good state or an average state. You should be nearly bouncing off the walls because you are so excited. Start doing some jumping jacks or do a little dance— whatever it takes. Now, grab a pen and paper, and find some space where you can be by yourself.

Become clear on what you want: Make a list of goals you have for your life, and separate them in the following categories: long-term goals, short-term goals, personal goals, family goals, health goals, spiritual goals, business/career goals, financial goals, social goals, hobby goals, and everything in between.

Since our objective with this book is to overcome any fear or shyness that has been holding us back, it is important to include the goal of the new, social, confident, peaceful person that you intend to become, but do not limit yourself there. Do not hold back.

Your top five: From those goals, choose five that are the most exciting to you. That is how you know you got the right ones. At least one of them should be reflective of the social, confident person that you are becoming during this journey. Once you have chosen your five, find images that represent what that goal looks like to you.

Make it real: Now we are going to bring those images to life and print them out. You can either make a vision board or use notecards, or both, and strategically place the board or cards in locations where you will see them every day (e.g., by your computer, in your car, attached to the mirror in the bathroom, on your phone as wallpaper, etc.).

Attached affirmations: For each goal, you are going to write down an affirmation as if the goal has already happened. The more specific you can be about exactly what you want and when you want it, the better the chances are that your brain can provide those answers. Effective affirmations are positive statements, charged with feeling, written in present tense, first person, beginning with "I am..." (e.g., "I am a confident, vibrant person who loves to socialize!")

See, feel, and believe them every day: The purpose of setting goals is not for the attainment of the goal itself. It is who you must become in the process, in order to be worthy of the desired outcome.

What we are doing to our subconscious mind when we look at each image, affirm it with certainty, and feel it in our body, is creating the emotion and belief we associate with that goal, which strengthens the magnetic force within you and guides you to where you need to be.

The reason why affirmations do not work for many people is that they fail to create the energy associated with the goal. Do not be a boring adult while you affirm these statements. Read or say them out loud if you can, with energy, passion, and joy. Place the notecards or vision board near your bed so you can look at the images and read the images first thing in the morning and right before you go to sleep.

You might be wondering, "Why am I setting goals? I thought this was about overcoming my fear and shyness." Great question. In the same way that a smoker cannot stop smoking until he creates a new habit, you will not be able to overcome your fear and shyness unless you are focused on projects or goals that you will be too excited about to be scared or shy.

I know this sounds strange, but I have experienced it in my own life, and if I can do it, I know for certain that you can do it too. Once you have set your goals and have them placed where you will see and feel them every day, it is time for you to get real and move on.

Who You Spend Time With Is Who You Become

Remember when we were younger, and our parents, teachers, and coaches would warn us and say, "I do not think it is good for you to be spending so much time with so-and-so; he/she is a bad influence on you." If you were like me, you probably ignored their advice and hung out with that person anyway.

Well, it turns out they were onto something. The late personal development guru, Jim Rohn, famously said, *"You become like the five people you spend the most time with. Choose carefully."*

Have you been choosing carefully lately? Either those five people are stretching and challenging you to become a social and confident person, or their complacency, fear, or shyness is rubbing off on you. Whether you like it or not, you are always being influenced by the people you choose to spend time with.

I am not saying that it is completely their responsibility, because you are the one who decided to spend time with them. They are behaving in the best way that they know how.

People change, and friends come and go. You do not have to stay friends with people who are constantly putting you down and keeping you stuck in bad habits and negative thinking. Take a look at your current friends, relatives, and role models, and ask yourself if these people are good for you. If not, limit the amount of time you spend with them.

Like I said, this change is not as easy to make as some of the other strategies we will talk about later. I am not suggesting that you start completely cutting people out of your life, but it is important to start becoming aware of the people you spend time with, and make the conscious effort to surround yourself with those who will influence you to become who you want to be.

Hang out with people with the same goals as you, who will be supportive and nonjudgmental.

How Do Others Influence Us?

Because of our human desires to connect and bond, we adopt the philosophy, habits, attitudes, standards, and lifestyle of those around us.

We like people who are like us, right? If most of your friends believe that people are scary, and that social situations are awkward, it is no surprise that you most likely will think this way too.

On the other hand, however, what if you had the type of friends who loved meeting new people and diving deep into conversations? How would you think differently? Which of your beliefs would change? How would you perceive others on a daily basis?

This was a huge shift for me. I had always been afraid to speak up or introduce myself because I believed that others would judge me—probably because I was constantly judging myself—but when I started spending more time with social people, I learned that people are not that scary at all.

By observing my extroverted friends sparking up conversations, I saw how good it made others feel to be recognized. Most of us walk around each day with an invisible sign around our necks that says, "Notice me! Make me feel important or special." Social people naturally use the mirror-out technique, and it has become a habit for them to start and engage in conversations.

Surrounding yourself with social people is so powerful because you adapt to their level of consciousness. It does not take a lot of willpower since you are subconsciously picking up their patterns and behavior.

Find Mentors and Role Models

Like I mentioned, you do not want to simply start cutting off those people from your life who you do not believe are contributing to your growth. Everyone has something special about him or her, and you have the power to bring that uniqueness out of them.

You will need to make the conscious effort to start surrounding yourself with mentors and role models who exemplify the characteristics that you want. There are two types that you want to connect with: direct and indirect mentors.

Direct mentors are the people you already know, who process the skills and attitudes that you want to adopt. These could be a leader at your job, a coach, a teacher, a community leader, or even a peer or friend.

If you are having a tough time thinking of people like this near you, do not worry. We live in the greatest time in human history for connecting with like-minded people, and at the end of this book, I will show you how to find them instantly.

Indirect mentors are people you aspire to become like and have a lot of respect for. It does not matter if this person is dead or alive, or lives close to you or in another state or country. It could be a professional athlete, artist, author, speaker, philanthropist, entrepreneur, or anyone else. There are no limits here.

I believe that I became so hooked on reading and listening to audios from successful people because it felt like we were sitting in the same room next to each other, and he or she was giving me all of their secrets. I did not have to go out and learn all of life's lessons through my own experiences; I could learn from them.

You have the same opportunity.

Well, congratulations. We have come to the end of the first half of the book, which has been all about changing your mindset, your breakthrough, and getting out of your comfort zone. Now we will move into the WOW part—techniques and strategies—to start harnessing their power for you! So, let us get started...

Be sure to visit YourTrueSelfBook.com, and click on FREE BOOK BONUSES to receive several valuable gifts, which include:

A full page, full color, print-ready copy of all *Your True Self Tips*.
A full page, full color, print-ready action plan!
The book, *Become Your True Self,* on audio, read by the author!

* Please note that the bonus offerings may change.

Notes

Notes

Chapter 5

Your Smile

*"Smiling breaks your pattern of negative thoughts,
and enforces your brain to start searching for memories, ideas,
and events that make you feel good."*
– Elan Sun Star

We made it! The first section of this book can be difficult because it requires us to take a good, hard look at ourselves in the mirror, and it is not always easy to see what is really going on.

Now I am going to share with you the exact techniques and strategies, called *Your True Self Tips,* which you can use out in the real world to break free and conquer your fear and shyness once and for all. These are trial-tested tactics and are proven through my own, and many others', experiences.

Think about this time that you spend each day reading and learning as you practice, as if you were playing a sport. When you are not reading, it is game time! You get to put these strategies to work and try them out. You may make some mistakes, but that is okay. Be open and patient with yourself, and trust that with practice and persistence, you will continue to improve.

We will focus on progress, not perfection. So, let us lace up and buckle down—we have work to do.

From Fear to Smiles

While I was in the honeymoon phase of overcoming my fear and shyness, a crazy idea came to me. One morning, for whatever reason, I decided that I would simply smile at each person I walked by. You can imagine the thoughts that popped up in my mind the first couple of days I would do this: "You look like such a fool! Stop smiling, you idiot! People are going think you are so weird!"

Whenever those thoughts would arise, I reminded myself that upwards of 95% of the population have the same fear and shyness as me. I would then shift my focus back and look for the next person I could share a smile with.

To my surprise, 99% of the people would smile back. That gave me the satisfaction that maybe, even just for a moment, I had the power to help make someone else's day a little better.

After a couple of weeks of my new smiling routine, I was ready to take this challenge to the next level. I started to add a "Good morning" to each person that passed me by. Again, it blew my mind what a positive response I would get back from people.

You might be thinking, "Well, of course, people would respond this way." Well, here is where this new little habit became transformative for me. By the time I would get to work or class, I would feel really good. For the first time, I was willing to get to work—to make friends and not hide from people.

Conquering my fear started with a smile. Yes, a simple smile. And here is how it can do the same for you.

Science of a Smile

As over simplistic and elementary as this first strategy is, it has the power to boost your confidence instantly, and research will back this up. You can find hundreds of studies that provide evidence for the benefits of smiling, even when you do not feel like it. But to me, it comes down to this one, simple truth. We cannot feel good and bad at the same time. It is just not possible.

Elan Sun Star, photographer and author of the book, *Smile! The Secret Science of Smiling,* wrote, *"Your mental and emotional state is affected by the state of your body, and vice-versa. So, if you make a change in one, you make a change in the other, because there is a mind-body-spirit continuum."*

"Smiling breaks your pattern of negative thoughts and focuses your brain to start searching for memories, ideas, and events that make you feel good."

We cannot expect to confidently talk to people if we do not feel good on the inside. Up to this point, I would guess that you associate pain and uncomfortable feelings with talking to people. It is only human nature for us to avoid pain and increase pleasure. It is easier to remain quiet and keep our thoughts to ourselves.

Remember when we talk about creating your breakthrough? We agreed that you would need to change your state of mind. Nothing will change your state faster than smiling, even if you need to force it at first.

The Hard Truth

We all need to take the social plunge. When I am in a social situation where I know I could potentially become fearful and anxious, I make the conscious effort to start smiling. Instantly, my stress is reduced, and I am able to stay in the moment—instead of being trapped in my mind—to keep my mirror pointing outward and to engage in the conversation.

You might be thinking, "Well, sure, but I do not want to be a phony person by faking smiles for the rest of my life." I understand. But I am willing to bet that after forcing a smile on your face for five seconds, it will not be fake anymore. You will actually start to feel better, and it will transform into a real smile.

You will start to give off a different type of energy when you walk around with a smile. Not only will you feel good but you will start to make others feel good too. A win-win!

Your Smile Attracts

As you start to smile more, you will notice that other people will begin initiating conversations with you more often, because they will be attracted to your good vibes and become curious about what makes you so happy.

Although this is something that might have terrified us before, now we have nothing to fear. In a later chapter, I will give you the most practical advice for what to say when you get to that point.

Carrying on through your day with a smile lets people know that you are safe. Instinctively, people want to protect themselves. Without words, your smile says to others, "Hey, it is okay! I am safe. I am not out to hurt you."

Before I started constantly practicing the smile strategy, I would walk with low energy and very little expression on my face, out of fear. As a result, I was left alone, and I liked it that way because I believed that hiding in my little shell was easier than facing my fear and opening up to others.

We can try to convince ourselves that we are happier by isolating ourselves from others and avoiding vulnerability, but it is just not the truth. We will begin to connect with more people and experience life in a much more rich and meaningful way when we smile and allow ourselves to be seen.

Practice, Practice, Practice

As silly as this sounds, you are going to need to practice your smiling on a daily basis. If you are not sure where to begin without feeling like an absolute fool, start by practicing around your house.

Smile when you are washing the dishes, smile when you are making coffee, smile when you are in the shower, smile while you do your laundry, and while you do everything else. As often as possible, smile!

And do not use the muscles around your mouth to give a half-hearted smile. There are hundreds of muscles in your face. Use them all. Smile so big that you can make the corners of your eyes crinkle.

If you live with your spouse, family, or roommates, they undoubtedly will think you are a crazy person at first. That is okay. Let them borrow the book, and encourage them to take a few minutes to read this chapter so they understand why you are doing it.

Once you are ready to take it to the next level, mindfully begin smiling when you go outside to walk your dog, get the mail, take out the trash, and when you do everything else.

Finally, start this smiling practice when you are at work, at school, on the bus, waiting in line at the restaurant, and everywhere else.

This will feel awkward at first. Please remember the simple fact of life: others are not thinking about, and/or judging, you as much as you think they are. Most people are too preoccupied with their own lives to be thinking about you. When I realized this, I was set free from my mind, and you can experience this liberation too.

If your mind starts to give you every reason why you should not practice smiling, thank it for its concern about your safety, but then give yourself permission to feel the incredible sensations of a huge, big smile. In the next chapter, you will learn an even more exciting *True Self Tip* to overcome your fear and shyness.

Be sure to visit YourTrueSelfBook.com, and click on FREE BOOK BONUSES to receive several valuable gifts, which include:

A full page, full color, print-ready copy of all *Your True Self Tips.*
A full page, full color, print-ready action plan!
The book, *Become Your True Self,* on audio, read by the author!

* Please note that the bonus offerings may change.

Notes

Notes

Notes

Chapter 6

Your Body Language

"Body language is a very powerful tool. We had body language before we had speech, and apparently, over 80% of what you understand in a conversation is read through the body, not the words."
– Deborah Bull

Similar to the smile muscles that you are developing and practicing from the last chapter, your second *True Self Tip* is your body language. Here is good news for people like you and me: 55% of communication is through our nonverbal clues, and 38% is our vocal inflection, leaving just 7% for the actual words we speak.

If you are like me, at times, you get worried that the words you speak are going to come out the wrong way. Knowing those percentages, it took away that pressure of getting the words right, so all I had to do was focus on improving my body language.

I am going to teach you a simple and easy-to-remember technique that you can use anytime you are in any social setting, and your confident body language will actually make you feel more confident. Are you ready? You don't want to miss this one.

As Easy as ABC

You are going to love these ABCs because you will see an immediate difference in the energy you bring to any conversation. It will work if you are meeting someone for the first time, talking to your boss or professor, with a group of friends, or anything else. All you need to remember are your ABCs, which stand for:

A – Adjust your shoulders
B – Breathe deeply and release
C – Clasp your hands
D – Display your smile
E – Eye contact

I cannot count how many times the ABCs have saved me in potentially uncomfortable social situations. Whenever my nerves start to rattle and my heart starts racing, I resort back to this powerful strategy.

It only takes about 10 seconds to make the adjustment as you go through this sequence. So, let us break down each of these…

Adjust Your Shoulders

Allowing our shoulders to drive forward and slouch over gives the perception to others that we lack confidence, decisiveness, and even sincerity.

Now, I know you are a sincere person, but your body language might suggest something different. The answer is simple. All you need to do is stand up straight, pull your shoulders back, and open your chest. No need to go all Superman or Wonder Woman with this one—just a subtle shift of the shoulders.

Let me be honest with you: I have had an extremely tough time staying true to this habit. My best friends were constantly reminding me to stand up straight and stop slouching. At first, this really bothered me. But they were absolutely right, and their reminders have helped me to make progress.

If your posture needs some work, I would suggest asking your partner, friends, or co-worker to call you out every time you are slouching. It will make all the difference in the long run.

Breathe Deeply and Release

Now that your shoulders are pulled back and your chest is open, take a deep breath, hold it for a few seconds, and exhale in a long sigh; then repeat one more time. When you exhale, imagine that all the tension in your body, and the worry in your mind, are being expelled.

If you are all tight and tensed up, the person you are talking to will subconsciously recognize those clues and know that you are feeling uncomfortable. Taking two deep breaths will begin to calm your nerves and help you return to the present moment so you can stay focused on the person and conversation.

Clasp Your Hands

Do you ever feel uncomfortable because you do not know what to do with your hands? I do. A simple adjustment in the positioning of your hands can make all the difference in the world.

One of the most common mindless habits we have when talking to someone is that we become all fidgety with our hands. While talking, do you ever touch your face, eyes, or hair? Do you ever adjust your clothes or jewelry? Again, the person you are talking to will subconsciously recognize those cues and know that you are feeling uncomfortable.

Although this part of the sequence is called *Clasp Your Hands,* there are a couple of different options you can choose from. However, as a general rule of thumb, I would recommend keeping your hands up by your chest when speaking, and down by your lap when listening.

As far as the positioning of your hands goes, you can either have them clasped together or in steeple pose, where your fingertips are touching. I prefer the steeple pose because I think it gives off more of a calm and collected vibe, but ultimately, it is up to you.

Display Your Smile

This one is self-explanatory. When listening to others speak, make the conscious effort to give a simple smile and nod accordingly. You want the person to feel that you are not just listening but you are also engaged and interested. Put a smile on your face to feel good and help others feel good too.

Eye Contact

If you are like me and feel intimidated by the idea of looking at someone directly in the eye during conversation, I have good news for you. You do not have to... at first. I will explain what I mean by that in a moment.

It is important that the person you are talking to knows and feels that you are generally interested in what they are saying, and the quickest way to gain this trust is through eye contact.

During one of my English classes in high school, I remember this one teacher instructing us on how to make eye contact. She suggested looking at the person's nose, lips, or in between their eyebrows, until you feel comfortable making direct contact.

This is a great place to start, until you have built up the courage to connect with their eyes. And once you do, do not feel that you have to maintain eye contact. You can go back to nose, lips, or in between eyebrows, anytime you feel uncomfortable.

Now that you are smiling and exuding confident body language by doing your ABCs, you are in a great position to start learning your third *True Self Tip*—the best one yet!

Be sure to visit YourTrueSelfBook.com, and click on FREE BOOK BONUSES to receive several valuable gifts, which include:

A full page, full color, print-ready copy of all *Your True Self Tips*.
A full page, full color, print-ready action plan!
The book, *Become Your True Self,* on audio, read by the author!

* Please note that the bonus offerings may change.

Notes

Notes

Notes

Chapter 7

The Three-Foot Rule

"Sometimes, the people you think don't want to talk to you are the ones waiting for you to talk to them."
– Anonymous

With more than half the battle won by mastering your body language, it is time to utilize some of *Your True Self Tips,* which will help you actually start—you know— talking to people.

Chances are that if you are like me, you have become really good at avoiding conversations and hiding in your shell. Well, I have got exciting news. It is going to be a lot easier to start and carry on conversations than you thought. In no time, you can become a brilliant conversationalist, with these simple, powerful techniques.

The third technique to start using is the *Three-Foot Rule.* In simplistic terms, this means that you will make the conscious effort to spark up a conversation with anyone within about three feet of you.

If you have been fearful and shy for most of your life, I know what you are thinking: *This sounds scary.* It is okay to have that thought, but I want to encourage you to keep an open mind. Plus, I am going to show you how this is going to be much simpler than you think.

The Danger of Not Talking to Strangers

If your parents were like mine when you were a kid, they reminded you not to talk to strangers. This was great advice when we were young and naïve, but we are not little kids anymore. In fact, if we do not talk to strangers, who are all really just one conversation away from becoming a good friend, then we will go through life struggling with our career, relationships, and overall happiness.

One of our basic human needs is connection with others and the world around us. Trust me, I know how lonely and empty it feels when you do not have that connection, and I want to help you communicate *your true self* more effectively.

But what am I going to say? The majority of us do not talk to people we do not yet know; we are afraid of what they might think of us and/or we do not think we would know what to say.

I would bet that either just now as you have been reading this, or sometime in your life, you have thought about talking with someone but then instantly froze up as you tried to structure an opening sentence. I am guilty of having done this so many times. So, I am going to share with you a simple process that will guide you to executing the Three-Foot Rule.

The Four Magic Words

Are you ready to hear the absolute best, and proven, opening line to start a conversation?

"Hello. How are you?"

What? That's it? Yes. It is okay to be mad at me for how simple this is, but research backs it up. This is great news if you are worried about coming up with the perfect opening line.

I learned this trick from Vanessa Van Edwards, who is a behavioral investigator, and author of the bestselling book, *Captivate: The Science of Succeeding with People*. She says, *"This opening line is easy and effective. Don't drive yourself crazy coming up with something clever or witty. This has worked for me one hundred percent of the time."*

Those four words have stuck with me ever since, and I saw a huge difference when I started applying this to the Three-Foot Rule. Once you get the conversation started, you will want to make sure to…

Shake Their Hand

This is not just custom or protocol; there is a science behind it. As soon as your hands meet, both of you will release oxytocin in your bodies, which will strengthen your bond.

We will not dive too far into the handshake—though I would encourage you to Google it—but for the sake of simplicity, remember to keep your hands dry and your grip firm (neither too soft nor too aggressive).

Introduce Yourself

I like to keep my introduction as short and simple as possible, so that I can keep the conversation focused on the other person, and learn about them.

If I were at the gym, I might say, "Hey, how is it going? My name is Wright. What type of workout are you doing today?" If I was sitting on an airplane, I might say, "Good morning; how are you? My name is Wright. Are you going to Chicago for business or for pleasure? Or is that your home?"

Once they respond, you can continue to ask more questions. We have a whole chapter coming up soon to talk about the power of questions. You will instinctively know when the best time is to shake their hand and introduce yourself, so do not get caught up in saying the right words—remember, it is only 7% of communication— and follow the process in a specific order.

It is more important to simply get the conversation started than to say the perfect opening line.

Now that you have broken the ice and done the toughest part of the Three-Foot Rule, there are a couple of tricks you can keep up your sleeve to keep the discussion flowing smoothly.

Smile and Nod

These two techniques are lifesavers for my fellow introverts and me. We tend to freak ourselves out before a conversation has even started, because we think we need to know exactly what to say. That is not true at all.

My goal in every conversation is to effectively execute the 80/20 rule. I want to keep the other person talking for 80% of the time while I only speak for 20%. Why? Because—let us be honest—most people like to talk about themselves. Now, I did not say we like opening up and talking that much with strangers, but when we feel comfortable, we love to give our opinions and share our thoughts.

This is something we can use to our advantage in any conversation. While the other person is talking, gracefully smile and nod. Research has proven that this will keep your fellow conversationalist talking.

The late Frank Bettger, author of the bestselling book, *How I Raised Myself from Failure to Success in Selling,* once said, *"I no longer worry about being a brilliant conversationalist; I simply try to be a good listener. I noticed that people who do that are usually welcome wherever they go."*

So, use your listening skills to your advantage, and you will experience incredible conversations wherever you go.

Closing the Conversation

As you sense the conversation coming to an end, you want to ask the other person something about their future. It does not need to be a deep question; it can be as simple as...

"What are you up to the rest of the day?" Or, "What are your plans for the weekend?"

The purpose of this is to set yourself up for a smooth ending. As you shake their hand to say goodbye, you can say...

"It was great chatting with you, Raymond. Have a great time hiking with your family this weekend."

The last impression can be just as important as the first one. It reminds the other person that you truly care and you really were interested. It leaves you both with a good feeling about the interaction.

If the other person abruptly ends the conversation, do not take it personally. Maybe they want to connect with other people in the room, have an appointment to keep, or just have to use the restroom. Remember to smile and tell them it was nice talking with them.

You might be wondering, "What if I want to keep in touch and stay connected with them?" Great question.

The most effective strategy, I discovered, is asking if he or she is on Facebook. I ask this for two reasons...

The first reason is because there are billions of users on Facebook, and so the chances are good that they are. The second reason is because I doubt I would ever text or call this person out of the blue. That comes off a little creepy to me and could potentially send mixed signals, especially if the person is of the opposite gender.

If they are on Facebook and want to connect on there, I always let them type in their name on my phone—it is faster that way—and again, it strengthens the trust and bond between us, since most of us cherish our phone as if it keeps us on life support.

Do not worry if they do not have a Facebook account, or if they do not want to stay connected. That rarely happens, and even if it does, you can still be thankful for the conversation and opportunity to strengthen your confidence muscle.

You can now successfully execute the Three-Foot Rule anytime, anywhere. Do not feel obligated to do it all the time, but I want to challenge you to start doing it once a day, or even just once a week at first.

Once you have done the toughest part—initiating the conversation— you are going to need to know how to ask good questions. This is one of my favorite topics to teach during my workshops, and my students get many ideas out of it. I will dive into this strategy in the next chapter.

Be sure to visit YourTrueSelfBook.com, and click on FREE BOOK BONUSES to receive several valuable gifts, which include:

A full page, full color, print-ready copy of all *Your True Self Tips.*
A full page, full color, print-ready action plan!
The book, *Become Your True Self,* on audio, read by the author!

* Please note that the bonus offerings may change.

Notes

Notes

Notes

Chapter 8

Ask Good Questions

"Ask the right questions,
and the answers will always reveal themselves."
– Oprah Winfrey

If you only take away one good *true self tip* from this book, then this is the one you want to highlight, underline, and start implementing immediately.

Remember how I mentioned earlier that you want to keep the other person talking for 80% of the interaction, and you will become a brilliant conversationalist? This is how you do it...

Ask questions!

I learned the power of this technique the day I had my breakthrough, and my whole life began to change. I started to become very curious about what exactly I was afraid of. Since my biggest fear was other people and remaining calm in a conversation, I started asking other people as many questions as I could think of.

What you will begin to discover is that you will learn a lot from other people, and a lot about yourself. The ultimate outcome from asking questions is finding common ground with the person you are speaking with. Many of us feel fearful, shy, and isolated because we do not believe that other people can relate to what we are feeling.

Well, guess what? We all have something in common!

Generally speaking, we all want to feel loved, we all have our fears, we all want to feel accepted, and we all want more out of at least one area of our life. With enough digging and sincere curiosity, we can connect with any given person, from anywhere in the world. Your purpose for asking questions in a conversation is to find that connection and build upon it.

The Power of a Question

One day, while I was on my way to do one of my workshops, I was standing in line at a local Starbucks to get a cup of coffee. In front of me was a man in his early thirties, with his three young boys, who were running and jumping in every direction. His face held the expression of exhaustion from trying to keep up with his kids but also of genuine joy and love for them.

Finally, I asked him this question: "What is the best part about being a father?"

He was completely thrown off and looked puzzled by the question. He stopped and pondered for a good five seconds before answering:

"Their unconditional love; it is the type of love that cannot be put into words." He then sincerely smiled at me as he walked up to the cashier to order his drink. Then he turned to me and asked what I was going to have, and after I answered, he paid for my coffee too.

After I thanked him and told him that he didn't need to do that, he said, "Thank you for making my day," as he left with his three sons, with a big smile on his face.

I have never forgot the way his face lit up after answering that question. Paying for my coffee was extremely generous but what was far more valuable was the lesson he taught me. We all have the power to make another person feel noticed, grateful, or appreciative by asking the right question.

What Types of Questions Should You Ask?

The depth of your questions will depend on your relationship with the other person. You may not want to ask someone, "What is the purpose of your life?" the first time you meet him or her. On the flipside, you probably do not want to be asking the person you have been dating or have been married to for three years, "What do you like to do for fun?" or something like that.

Here are some of my favorite questions to ask someone I am still getting to know...

- What are you passionate about?
- What is your family like?

- Who is your favorite historical figure?
- What is your story?
- What is the best part about being a parent?
- If you could have lunch with anyone, dead or alive, who would it be, and why?
- If money were no object, how would you really spend each day?
- If you could visit anywhere in the world, where would you go, and why?
- Have you read a book that completely changed your perspective?

These types of questions go beyond the surface level and give you the chance to learn more about a person's *true self,* without making them feel uncomfortable. If those questions seem a little too much for you, scale it down and start with the basics...

What do you do for a living?
Where did you go to school?
Where did you grow up?
Where is your favorite place to eat?
What is your favorite movie?
Who is your best friend?
What is the best vacation you have ever been on?

Again, what you are saying is less important than the fact that you are engaged in the conversation and are continuously asking questions that stimulate the other person's mind. Just keep asking questions and then comment on what the other person says.

That is all you need to do in a good conversation. And if an awkward silence threatens to put an untimely end to the conversation, have some ready-to-go questions to fill in.

Be an Active Listener

What most people do, while the other person is talking, is think about what they are going to say next. If you have a habit of doing this, make the decision right now that you are going to work on quieting your mind and being fully present and actively listening while the other person speaks.

The five elements of active listening are…

Provide positive feedback, both verbally and nonverbally. Verbal feedback can be, "I see," "Yeah," "Gotcha," etc. Nonverbal feedback includes looking them in the eyes, smiling, and giving appropriate facial expressions and gestures.

Ask questions to clarify what you are hearing. If you are not sure about the meaning of a speaker's words, ask clarifying questions, such as, "What do you mean by that?" Be sure the speaker understands that your intentions are to seek clarification rather than to challenge.

Reword what the speaker is saying to see if you understand them correctly. Preface your rewording with such comments as, "So, if I understand you correctly, you are saying… (state what you think they said, in your own words) Is that right?"

Avoid interrupting. Keep silent, except for verbal feedback or asking a clarifying question, until they are completely finished. Then give your responses, ignoring any emotional argument they may have used, and focus only on the facts and logic.

Be open-minded and tolerant; plus, express neither agreement nor disagreement. In your role as a listener, it is more important to clearly understand the speaker than to indicate whether or not you agree or disagree with them. That way, you can usually get more of the truth behind their words. Once you know their truth, you can come to some understanding.

What you will discover, as you begin to practice this, is that you learn a lot more about a person from the emotion behind their words, rather than from just their words alone. Start paying attention to the other person's body language. If you notice the emotion does not align with the words they speak, start asking more questions about it.

Have you ever watched the long-running TV show, *Criminal Minds*? I love the philosophy behind it and the way the profilers observe people's behavior. We do not have to work for the Behavioral Analysis Unit of the FBI to use this technique to start noticing the truth behind people's words. As we keep our mirror pointed out, we will be given clues on what types of questions to ask next.

We cannot get better at this skill simply by reading this book, or even by attending one of my workshops. We have to put this technique into everyday use.

The next time you are out in public, ask at least one person a question. Notice your surroundings, find common ground, and spark up a conversation. It is okay if your interaction is short and does not go anywhere; this is more about you developing these new skills and facing your fears.

Now, to put this all together and ensure sustainable success with your communication skills, we are going to need to incorporate these skills with what we are going to talk about in the next chapter—the last and most exciting of *Your True Self Tips.*

Be sure to visit YourTrueSelfBook.com, and click on FREE BOOK
BONUSES to receive several valuable gifts, which include:

A full page, full color, print-ready copy of all *Your True Self Tips.*
A full page, full color, print-ready action plan!
The book, *Become Your True Self,* on audio, read by the author!

* Please note that the bonus offerings may change.

Notes

Notes

Notes

Chapter 9

The Five-Second Rule

"You have a five-second window in which you can move from idea to action, before your brain starts to sabotage you."
– Mel Robbins

There is a very good chance that you have already heard one or more of these techniques and strategies you just read about. Sometimes we simply need to hear it from a different perspective and from someone else's story.

I have given you the blueprint to get in the right mindset, as well as these *True Self Tips,* which have been proven by hundreds of thousands of people to overcome their fear and shyness, and improve social skills.

This last technique is an idea that you may not have heard of before, and I believe it is the secret sauce to actually make this all work for you. How many times have you known what to do, and even how to do it, but you still did not follow through? How often have you had an idea of what you could say to spark a conversation with someone who looks interested, but you held back and hid in your shell instead?

Well, your days of self-sabotage have ended—now.

How to Stop Screwing Yourself Over

This was the title of a TED talk, where Mel Robbins, of CNN, introduces what she calls *The Five-Second Rule.* This is not about picking up food off the ground and eating it within five seconds. It is, as she suggests, that we all already know what we want, but knowing is not enough. It is just not as simple as the *Just Do It* slogan; otherwise, we would all be living the life of our dreams already.

The reason we do not is because when our feelings and our thoughts are up against each other in the moment of decision, our feelings always win. Sound familiar?

I really want to make new friends in class; I just do not have the courage to introduce myself.
I really want to speak up in our weekly meetings at work; I just do not feel like it.
I really want to ask that girl out on a date; but what if she says no?

Our feelings can be either our best friend or our worst enemy, depending on the action that we take. Knowing what to do, and knowing why you want to do it, will never be enough. So, what is the solution?

In Mel Robbins' words, *"If you have an impulse to act on a goal, you must physically move within five seconds, or your brain will kill the idea."*

Start the countdown once you get the impulse, and then take action!

What Does This Look Like in Real Life?

When you see that person you have been wanting to meet, you start the countdown... 5... 4... 3... 2... 1... Say hi, and introduce yourself!

When your boss asks if anyone has any ideas for the upcoming project, you start the countdown... 5... 4... 3... 2... 1... Speak up!

There are hundreds and hundreds of opportunities each day, where you can use this Five-Second Rule to overcome your fear/shyness, and become a more effective communicator. Ralph Waldo Emerson, an American essayist, lecturer, philosopher, and poet of the mid-19th century, is quoted as saying, *"Do the thing, and you will have the power. But they that do not do the thing, have not the power."*

No more pondering and contemplating the life you want to live and the person you want to become. The power and magic will start to happen when we go for it.

No matter how many books we read, audios we listen to, or seminars we attend, nothing changes until we do the thing. If we wait until we have the courage or motivation, we will be waiting the rest of our lives.

If you let it, this secret sauce can transform your entire life, because it is grounded in taking action!

My Own Twist

When I first learned about Mel Robbins' simple yet incredible effective strategy, I saw immediate results. When I am out running errands and feel the urge to share a compliment or ask a question to a stranger, I begin the countdown. When I need to make a call for my business that I have been avoiding, I begin the countdown.

However, I made a slight adjustment to it. I noticed that five seconds was a little too much time to give my brain before I would go back into panic mode and talk myself out of it. I decided to cut the time down to three seconds, and it worked like a charm.

I am not going to sit here and pretend that I am perfect with this technique—or any of the other ones that I have also given to you. I still let my fear get the best of me once in a while, and I hold back. But I do not beat myself up about it anymore because I know that this is a lifetime commitment to improvement—which we will talk about in the next chapter.

Right here, right now, think about something you have been wanting to do for a while now but keep putting off. It does not need to be a grand gesture like giving a speech or anything like that. It can literally be as simple as making plans with a friend, or telling someone you are sorry, or even cleaning your house or car.

Once you have locked in what you need to do, put down this book, and start the countdown... 5... 4... 3... 2... 1... Go!

If you start to doubt yourself with, "Yeah, but…," then start the countdown over again! Do not wait another minute. Do it now, and start practicing this—especially in social situations—as much as possible.

This technique will help you see instant progress in your conversation skills. But you have to remember that this is a lifetime commitment to growth. In the next and last chapter, we are going to put this all together—the WOW moment! So, let us quickly get into it.

Be sure to visit YourTrueSelfBook.com, and click on FREE BOOK
BONUSES to receive several valuable gifts, which include:

A full page, full color, print-ready copy of all *Your True Self Tips.*
A full page, full color, print-ready action plan!
The book, *Become Your True Self,* on audio, read by the author!

* Please note that the bonus offerings may change.

Notes

Notes

Notes

Chapter 10

Lifetime Commitment of Your New Life

"You always have two choices: your commitment versus your fear."
– Sammy Davis, Jr.

Did you actually do the Five-Second Rule from the last chapter? How did it go? How do you feel? If not, put this book down, and go do it right now! Let me remind you that the purpose of this book is to start taking action so you can make the changes to become more of *your true self.*

Assuming you have done it and started using the other *True Self Tips* in your daily life, we can move forward, as this journey together is coming to an end... for now.

There Is No Finish Line

Over the years, I have read many books and have listened to thousands of hours of audio in the areas of personal and human development. Bookstores, and Amazon, put many of these books in the category of self-help, but I like to think of it as self-discovery. I needed that constant reminder of ideas and strategies that would help me detach from believing in the negative thoughts that would creep into my consciousness.

I am sharing this, not to brag or boost my ego but to encourage you to commit to a lifetime of discovering yourself through books and audios that can change your mindset, and ultimately, your life.

I like to think of the ideas, from the books and audios, as being seeds planted in my brain. Growth occurs when I take action on the ideas from a book. Action is like rain and sunshine: without it, seeds will not sprout and grow. I never know when the harvest will come, but when it does, it feels amazing.

I hope you go back and read this book again, and share it with your friends, but I am also hopeful that you will seek out other authors, speakers, and people who have the skills, knowledge, and insight that you want to develop. Make sure you also go to my website and download the FREE bonuses!

The great Albert Einstein always said, *"Once you stop learning, you start dying."*

The irony is that I used to hate reading. I was an average student and got through school by skimming through books. My self-esteem, confidence, and inner-peace started to increase once I realized that learning is not about memorizing facts—it is, instead, a journey of becoming aware of ourselves and strengthening our minds.

A Story to Remember

A person I think about nowadays, who motivates me as a role model, and should motivate you too, is Abraham Lincoln. If anyone could have used an excuse of why he could not do it, it was Abe.

Abe never got past the first grade in formal education because he had to help his father on the farm, each and every day. His father did not believe in education, and because of this, his father could not read or write. But Abe's passion was to become a lawyer. He was admitted to the bar in 1836, when he was 26 years old.

So, how could anyone become a lawyer without going to law school, let alone having only one year of formal education? Everyone else would have excuses of why not, but Lincoln did not. And while everyone told him he was nuts, and the odds were stacked against him, Lincoln self-taught himself through books.

Fast forward to 1858, when Abe ran for the United States Senate, and lost. Two years later, he ran for President of the United States, against that same person who he lost to in the Senate race... and won.

People were telling him again that he was nuts, and that the odds were stacked against him, and that he was going to lose. And the list of his life could go on all day.

His son, Robert Todd Lincoln, while speaking at the dedication of the Lincoln Memorial, stated this quote that his father told him often when he was growing up: *"You can be successful or you can make excuses. But remember, you can't do both."*

So, if you are going to overcome your fear and shyness, you need to take action.

The Entertainment Thing

I still remember to this day, back in 1966, when my father brought home our family's first color TV. It only had a twelve-inch screen, and the back of the set went out two feet, to hold the tube. Boy, how things have changed.

Anyway, the reason for this story is, anytime we had dinner, or breakfast, or lunch, after school, or on weekends, the TV was always on. It was a great way for me not to talk to anyone, and even more detrimental to reading or doing schoolwork. Hey, watching *Bozo's Circus, The Flintstones, The Jetsons, Here's Lucy*, etc., was a lot more fun and easier for me. I digress.

I know for a fact now that TV was a big reason I did not like to read while growing up. Research has shown that long-term effects of watching TV include lowering verbal reasoning ability, as well as physical, mental, and emotional development. Having figured this out, I hardly ever turn the TV on. It was just wasting away my brain and life anyway.

As for books, reading keeps the mind mentally alert as you age, and it also lowers stress. Research even found that Alzheimer's is 2.5 times less likely to appear in people who read regularly, while TV was presented as a huge risk factor. The biggest difference comes in communication. Research has shown that readers are more willing to talk, while TV viewers are more likely to stay quiet in their shell.

Of course, the bigger culprit, nowadays, is that smart phone we all have; and unfortunately, research is showing the same exact trends between phones and TV. So, the bottom line is that reading will help you tremendously as you break out of your fear and shyness. It has for me, and it will for you too.

The Next Step

My invitation to you is simple. I am asking you to commit to a lifetime of personal development so that you can become the best version of yourself that you can be. In other words, *Become Your True Self.*

I want you to start envisioning your life once you have overcome your fear and shyness. Who do you want to be? What do you want to do? Where do you want to go? What kind of legacy do you want to leave behind for your family and the world around you? If we are only focused on overcoming fear and shyness, we are vulnerable to remaining stuck in that illusion for longer than we would like.

We only have one shot at this thing called life, my friend, and even if you believe in reincarnation, I think it is about time you get off the wheel of birth, mediocrity of life, and death. I am certain that you have talents, abilities, and gifts that the world needs to witness. I am giving you permission to be yourself in a world that tries to label and define you as you are supposed to be.

Do not give in. Be bold and unapologetically *you,* in your pursuit and commitment to live a life that you can be proud of. I believe in you! And I look forward to meeting you in person soon.

5... 4... 3... 2... 1... You got this!

Be sure to visit YourTrueSelfBook.com, and click on FREE BOOK
BONUSES to receive several valuable gifts, which include:

A full page, full color, print-ready copy of all *Your True Self Tips.*
A full page, full color, print-ready action plan!
The book, *Become Your True Self,* on audio, read by the author!

* Please note that the bonus offerings may change.

Notes

Notes

About the Author

Wright Chase, who was born and raised in Chicago, and still calls it home, has been an entrepreneur throughout his life. He knew, ever since high school, he needed to break out of his shell of fear and shyness, and get out of his comfort zone of not saying boo to anyone, if he was going to be successful. It has taken him many years to figure this out, and he is willing to share his techniques with you today.

Wright enjoys teaching other people his knowledge and wit, while having fun. Everyone needs to *Become Your True Self* and gain control of your awesome life that you can be proud of. You can do this, and Wright is willing to help.

The author is available for delivering workshop and keynote presentations to appropriate audiences. He guarantees to deliver an inspiring, heartfelt, and captivating experience for everyone in attendance. For rates and availability, please contact the author directly, at: Wright@WrightChase.com

To order more books, please visit:
www.YourTrueSelfBook.com

Finally, if this book has inspired you, the best thing you could ever do is pass this on and be a wonderful role model for others.

Made in the USA
Monee, IL
09 November 2021